Sexuality
a catholic perspective

Teachers' Book

Brian Johnstone & Vanessa Rohan

Collins Dove, Melbourne, Australia.

Published by Collins Dove
60–64 Railway Road, Blackburn, Victoria, 3130, Australia
Tel: (03) 877 1333

Cover design by Shane Conroy
Design by Shane Conroy and Maryann Purcell
Revision editing by Adrian Lyons SJ
Typeset in 10/11 Baskerville by Bookset Pty Ltd
Printed in Australia by Globe Press, Brunswick, Victoria.

National Library of Australia Cataloguing-in-publication data:
Johnstone, B. (Brian) and Rohan, V. (Vanessa)
   Sexuality: a Catholic Perspective: teachers' book
   Bibliography.
   ISBN 0 85924 573 X
   1. Sex — Religious aspects — Catholic Church
   I. Rohan, Vanessa. II. Title
261.8'357

Photocredits
H. Birnstihl   pp 6, 24.   T. Lloyd   pp iv, 4, 26, 33, 38.
M. Coyne   p 36.   D. Lovell   pp 7, 28.
G. Horner   pp 2, 12, 14, 16.   D. Whyte   p 8.

Contents

For the educator

Why Sex Education?

Teachers, parents, youth leaders and others with an interest in sex education will know from experience some of the difficulties which can arise in this area. We believe, however, that these difficulties are outweighed by the positive value of fostering a deeper appreciation of personal sexuality. As the *Declaration on Certain Questions Concerning Sexual Ethics* by the Roman Catholic Sacred Congregation for the Doctrine of the Faith states '. . . it is from the sex that the human person receives the characteristics which, on the biological, psychological and spiritual levels, make that person a man or a woman, and thereby largely condition his or her progress towards maturity and insertion into society'. We are dealing, then, with aspects of life which must be 'honoured with great reverence'.

If we accept that education is meant to foster growth to maturity, then it must include education in sexuality. This was recognised explicitly by the Second Vatican Council in its *Declaration on Christian Education*: 'As they advance in years they [children and young people] should be given positive and prudent sexual education.'

The Educational Process

Granted that education in sexuality is necessary, what kind of educational process is appropriate? The process we have favoured in this book can be explained in terms of
(a) basic values and presuppositions
(b) organisational framework.

Basic values and presuppositions

A wide range of documents on education have emerged within the Catholic Church in recent times. In these documents a set of basic values and presuppositions are evident. Among these are:

1. Education should lead towards personal *responsibility*.
2. Education should provide aid towards achieving inner, moral *freedom* and towards choosing a definite attitude to life.
3. The young have to rely on themselves and *their own consciences*, and must assume responsibility for their own destinies.

It is our hope that these values may provide a meeting point for moral educators from different religious and philosophical backgrounds. Thus, while we have sought to present and explain the Catholic view of the issues raised, we have also tried to keep open avenues of dialogue with others.

Statement of Principles

Church guidance
In November 1983, the Sacred Congregation for Catholic Education issued a document entitled 'Educational Guidance in Human Love'. In the light of this document, some suggestions can be offered to help integrate material in this book with other important elements in the religious education program, and with the spiritual life of students.

1. In *Sexuality: A Catholic Perspective* we stress the positive features of the Catholic tradition. This is also the emphasis of the Sacred Congregation's document. At the same time, it is helpful to have clear statements about what is wrong in the area of sexuality. In particular, teachers need to know how a truly theological and relational understanding of sin (different from the popular meaning of 'sin') can be developed.

Key points made in the Sacred Congregation's document (hereafter referred to as EG) are these:

(a) Sexuality must be integrated into the whole life of a person, otherwise it can take on a disproportionate role. The ability to guide one's sexual instinct towards love and integrate it into one's whole personal development is a gift of God's grace. This integration is called chastity.[EG #18] The encyclical letter *Familiaris Consortio* expands this point: 'In the Christian view, chastity by no means signifies rejection of human sexuality or lack of esteem for it; rather it signifies spiritual energy capable of defending love from the perils of selfishness and aggresssion, and able to advance love towards its full realisation'. [EG#38] The process of personal development is made harder because our human frailty is weakened by sin, and because our culture is flawed. (See *Sexuality* Chapter 6.)

(b) An appreciation of the positive values should always come before any teaching about violations of them.[EG #36–38] This principle has been kept very much in mind throughout the book.

2. Teaching about sexuality should be integrated with teaching about the Sacraments and prayer.[EG #30] In the text we have suggested how teaching about the Sacrament of Matrimony could be related to this course. (See Chapter 8.) Some further points of integration could be:

(a) Baptism [EG #43]: Incorporated into the Risen Christ by this Sacrament, the Christian knows that his or her body has been enlivened and purified by the Spirit whom Jesus communicates. (See section 4 on 'the Christian tradition' in Chapter 1.) The implication of this belief is a deep reverence for the bodies of persons, one's own and others'.

(b) The word of God [EG #44]: Sin, which operates in the individual and in society, pressures a person to adopt ideas and ways of living their sexuality that are opposed to the law of Christ. (These points are underlined in *Sexuality* Chapters 1, 5, 6 and 8.) In particular, economic structures, some laws, the mass media and some aspects of city living can exert a

5

negative influence.[EG #44, 66, 68] Discovering what is involved in a truly human and Christian life, and actually living it out, can be greatly helped by familiarity with the Word of God received in faith, by prayer and through the Sacraments. [EG #45, 53] Throughout the book we have cited Scripture; we suggest that teachers discuss these passages with their students and encourage them to search for others relevant to the question.

(c) The Eucharist [EG #45]: The Eucharist is a communion with Christ in the sacrifice expressing his totally selfless love. It reveals the deepest meaning of love. (Christ's love could well be discussed with the class at various points of the book but especially in Chapter 4, concerning *agape*.)

The process of growing towards discovery — of oneself, of others and of God — is spoken about in Christian tradition as a journey. The Sacred Congregation's document explains that the believer can find in the Eucharist food for the journey, to give strength to overcome difficulties and to continue.

(d) The Sacrament of Reconciliation [EG #45]: In the text we have suggested ways in which Reconciliation might be related to the course. (See especially the end of Chapter 5.) The document explains that the Sacrament reinforces our capacity to resist evil and gives a person courage to stand up and continue after a fall.

(e) The sacramental community [EG #45]: Genuine love leads us out of isolation and into community. In the Church, the community of believers, we can find the necessary love and support. To gain this, we need to be actively involved in the community. (This is emphasised in *Sexuality* at the end of Chapter 6.) Active participation will involve a person in the sacramental and prayer life of the community, and also in an active apostolate — bringing the Good News to others through the way we live, as well as by our concern for justice and for the underprivileged.

(f) Prayer [EG #46]: Both personal and community prayer are necessary to us if we are to have the strength we need. Our human nature is wounded by sin and we are vulnerable to negative influences in our environment. (The role of prayer might well be addressed with the 'Discerning and deciding' section in Chapter 2.)

Prayer is a valuable path toward self-understanding. It is also a way to discover the presence of God in oneself and others, leading toward reverence for other persons. (A Christian's need for help — including prayer — to integrate emotions, feelings and action would form a natural part of class discussion of Chapter 6.)

(g) Devotion to Mary [EG #47]: Through centuries of experience, the faithful, and especially young people, have been much helped in achieving the ideal of a chaste Christian life through devotion to Mary. Teachers may find helpful Carlo Carretto's *Blessed are You who Believed*, Orbis Books, New York, 1983.

Personal responsibility

In this book we have tried to present accurately the values of the tradition and the present position of the Church. But ultimately decisions about life and personal relationships are a matter of *personal responsibility. So any genuine educational program must respect that responsibility and seek to develop it:*

. . . a true education aims at the formation of the human person with respect to his ultimate goal, and simultaneously with respect to the good of those societies of which, as a man, he is a member, and in whose responsibilities, as an adult, he will share.

As a consequence, with the help of advances in psychology and in the art of teaching, children and young people should be assisted in the harmonious development of their physical, moral and intellectual endowments. Surmounting hardships with a gallant and steady heart, they should be helped to acquire gradually a more mature sense of responsibility towards ennobling their own lives through constant effort, and towards pursuing authentic freedom.

Second Vatican Council, *Declaration on Christian Education.*

To be responsible a person must be *free*. In this program we are addressing people who are intelligent and free. We may present our views and even strongly argue a case, but we may never seek to infringe on their freedom:

It [the Catholic School] must develop persons who are responsible and inner-directed, capable of choosing freely and in conformity with their conscience.

Congregation for Catholic Education, *The Catholic School*

7

The educational process, then, is a process of exchange between free responsible persons. A responsible person seeks the true way; and so responsibility goes together with *conscience*. This book contains a special section on conscience and the relations between conscience and authority, but in fact *all* its discussions of values and decisions are addressed to conscience:

With youth comes the moment of the first great decisions. Although the young may enjoy the support of the members of their family and their friends, they have to rely on themselves and their own conscience and must ever more frequently and decisively assume responsibility for their destiny.

Pope John-Paul II, *Catechesis in Our Time.*

If the education process is an exchange between free, responsible persons, then we must respect the other persons involved. That will mean respecting the fact that not all may be at the same level of development. But why do students differ in their level of appreciation of moral issues? One important factor is the home and parent–child relationships. Where there has been a positive and rewarding relationship with parents a young person's response is likely to reflect an identification with the values of the parents. Recent studies have shown that this is likely to be the case whether parents are 'liberally' orientated, 'middle of the road' or 'conservative'.

Other studies have suggested that a young person's level of moral appreciation is raised through encounters with others using a higher level of moral reasoning. The level of moral appreciation shown by parents could thus be important for the child's moral development, with parents who approach moral questions at higher levels helping to stimulate their children to move up.

There is also the question of emotional conditioning. Where a parent qualifies people, places or types of behaviour with adjectives which have strong emotional connotations this

can have a powerful effect, influencing, for example, the way a child feels about persons of the other sex, about sexuality itself or about types of sexual behaviour.

Kohlberg's insights

The studies referred to above frequently advert to 'growth' or 'development', but without adopting any particular theory of development. Many teachers, parents and group leaders will be familiar with the work of Lawrence Kohlberg. Kohlberg's theory of moral development, despite the controversy it has generated, may still provide some help to teachers in the field of moral education. If nothing else it draws our attention to the reality of development and to the possibility that students or group members may be at different levels of development. This implies no reflection on their moral integrity; it simply means that their way of thinking about moral issues may be on a different level.

This has important practical consequences. We often tend to present moral arguments on a rather high level. The official Church statements quoted above all talk in terms of responsibility, freedom and conscience. But not everybody may have reached the level of understanding at which the meaning of the term 'conscience' can be fully appreciated. Teachers with experience in this area will recognise some of the difficulties here. 'That is a matter for conscience' is often interpreted as meaning 'That is a matter for arbitrary choice on the basis of whim or feeling'. On the other hand, if we say, 'There is a clear moral teaching and also a law on this matter', it will be taken to mean that there is no place for conscience at all. It is common for a group to be able to think only in terms of decisions based either on 'spontaneous feelings' or 'law', and often enough no amount of explanation seems to get us beyond this.

This is the kind of problem Kohlberg's theory can help us to understand. A person who is concerned above all with not breaking rules, with avoiding punishment and with not doing physical harm, could be at the *first stage* described by Kohlberg. A person who thinks about moral questions merely in terms of spontaneous feelings of like and dislike, for example, may be at *stage two* in Kohlberg's schema. At this stage personal satisfaction is seen as the key issue in a moral question.

Many of the young people with whom we talked in preparing this book recognised very clearly the influence of peer groups and 'what others think' on decision-making. Some people consider moral issues basically in terms of the approval or disapproval of others, a pattern of thinking identified in Kohlberg's schema as the *third stage*. Similarly, a person who was concerned above all with what parents or authority figures might think would be operating at this stage.

Another group of persons seem to think of moral questions above all in terms of law, and they may be at Kohlberg's *fourth stage* of moral development. This is the 'authority' stage. At this stage a person tends to think of the law as sacrosanct; it must be obeyed since it is sacred. Reasons are not important. One simply accepts the law and obeys it.

The *fifth stage* is marked by concern for consensus. For example, stealing would be judged wrong because it was against the democratically accepted law of society. The *sixth stage* is the stage of principles. A person at this stage follows principles which she or he has personally adopted.

According to Kohlberg, a person may move up through these various stages by being confronted with ways of thinking about moral questions which are one level above that at which he or she has been operating.

Kohlberg's theory has been criticised as too narrow in its focus, appearing to prize too highly moral judgement of a dispassionate and objective kind. Carol Gilligan, in her study entitled *In a Different Voice* (Harvard University Press, 1982) argues that Kohlberg, Erikson and other writers on moral development have tied their studies too closely to male development, failing to acknowledge the different perspectives of women. Her research shows that women prize *attachment* highly (the web of relationships) and perceive moral dilemmas as conflicts of personal responsibility. Men typically see moral maturity as a matter of *independence* (and prize a place in a hierarchy); their perception of moral dilemmas is less relational than that of women and more instrumental. Men's ethic is based on achievement, women's on care.

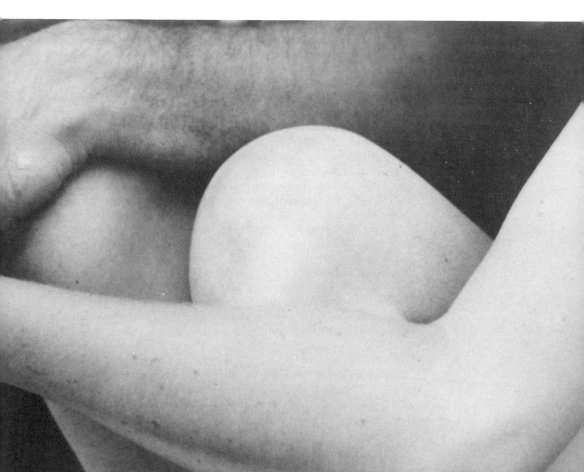

Gilligan cites as evidence the differing assessments made by Jake and Amy, two eleven-year-olds, about the appropriate action to take — and the reasons for it — in a case of a moral conflict: Should a man steal a $1000 drug to save his wife's life? Gilligan remarks about their responses:

These two children see two very different moral problems — Jake a conflict between life and property that can be resolved by logical deduction, Amy a fracture of human relationship that must be mended with its own thread. Asking different questions that arise from different conceptions of the moral domain, the children arrive at answers that fundamentally diverge, and the arrangement of these answers as successive stages on a scale of increasing moral maturity calibrated by the logic of the boy's response misses the different truth revealed in the judgment of the girl. To the question, 'What does he see that she does not?' Kohlberg's theory provides a ready response, manifest in the scoring of Jake's judgments a full stage higher than Amy's in moral maturity; to the question, 'What does she see that he does not?' Kohlberg's theory has nothing to say. Since most of her responses fall through the sieve of Kohlberg's scoring system, her responses appear from his perspective to lie outside the moral domain.

Gilligan's own conclusions have been criticised for drawing too sharp a contrast between men and women, rather than between the male and female characteristics shared in different proportions by individuals of the two sexes.

It is worth noting that there are Christians both in the Catholic Church and in Fundamentalist groups who place little importance on moral reasoning or on developmental perspectives. They believe that the Church's magisterium in one case, and the Bible in the other, manifest God's law in particular cases so clearly that there is no room for the believer, young or old, to do other than obey. Fundamentalists distrust human reason, including moral reason, regarding it as fatally flawed by the Fall. In the Catholic Church, the 'Natural Law' tradition, claiming that much can be discovered about God's intentions by all people of good will, claims St Thomas Aquinas and other medievals as its founders. The underlying belief of this tradition is that the Holy Spirit is active in guiding people of good will towards good and away from evil.

Whatever may be the final verdict on Kohlberg's and Gilligan's ideas, they do alert us to the possibilities of growth in moral reasoning and make us aware of the different levels at which people may be operating. If we are to respect others we must be prepared to recognise and accept them at the stage they have reached. For example, a teacher, parent or group leader may assert that something must be done simply because the authorities have said so, but evoke very little response. The reason may be that the persons to whom he is talking have moved beyond Kohlberg's fourth stage and are looking for more satisfying reasons for following moral rules.

Confusion or Clarity?

In recent years many teachers have felt uneasy at what they experience as confusion and uncertainty in the areas of values and morality. Thus we have sought to present clearly the official position of the Church. A simple assertion of the official position is not enough, however. A series of authoritative statements would in no way satisfy the type of education for which the official statements themselves call.

The educational process, particularly in the area of values, must be a dialogue of free, intelligent persons.

Value clarification, indoctrination or what?

The importance of educating people to make decisions of personal conscience is more and more recognised today. Initially value clarification strategies were often found helpful in this area. Students began to explore their own convictions and come up with their own decisions. But there were problems. Sometimes people arrived at ideas and decisions which seemed to others to be irresponsible and dangerous. Should these decisions be challenged and even contradicted? Or does that represent a return to 'indoctrination'? What about the responsibility we all have for unequivocal witness to the truth? May an educator challenge value choices which he or she believes to be inadequately formed?

If we take seriously recent work on moral development we come to see that these questions are less simple than they first appear. People may well be at different levels of development and respect for another person entails respect for the level of moral development she or he has reached.

For example, adults who tell adolescents to 'make up their own minds about pre-marital sex' are often imposing an impossible task. Acting under the illusion that they are free, young people may simply switch to such surrogate authorities as peers, television, movies, music and magazines.

An individual may often know, from personal experience or that of others, that certain forms of behaviour are really harmful. It is a betrayal of free, responsible dialogue to fail to state this. We do not show a respect for the integrity, intelligence and autonomy of others by refusing to express and defend our own well-founded convictions.

Whose values?

The moral tradition in which we have been formed carries the collective experience of generations. It condemns doing evil that good may come of it. It condemns dishonesty, injustice, exploitation. The tradition has something to say and there are reasons to support what it says.

For one who believes in Jesus Christ, the Scriptures and the traditions of the Christian Church bring a new, critical light to bear on moral questions. The moral guidance offered here is not a strange, unintelligible morality; it can be explained and

13

supported by reason. It can be shown to be a way to true and full humanity. Intelligent dialogue requires a believer to explore and convey these reasons.

For a person who is committed to the Catholic Church, the collective wisdom of the Catholic community, expressed by legitimate authority, has a special importance. However, the basis of the claims of that authority need to be explained. Not all authoritative statements have the same degree of authority. Out of respect for the genuine faith and intelligence of those involved we must try to make these points clear.

An important area in the Church's moral teaching about sexuality concerns *contraception*. Here the values at stake need to be carefully noted and explained. Catholic teaching on sexuality, while admitting the value of responsible parenthood, has always been against fertility control by artificial means, that is, by 'contraception'. It sees this as an unnatural intervention in a personal and life-giving relationship. The deep reasons for this, as *Sexuality: A Catholic Perspective* explains, are:
* the sacramental meaning of married love
* the responsible character of personal relationships
* the dignity of the human person
* respect for women, and
* a respect for the natural laws of biology.
Just as the larger ecology of nature has to be respected, so also has the ecology of our sexual being. Hence the Church has been a major promoter of 'natural methods' of fertility control.

14

Such teaching is to be found above all in *Humanae Vitae* (Of Human Life: 1968). Of course such teaching, together with bishops' statements applying it, reflections by moral theologians and the guidance of wise pastors and spiritual directors, recognises the complexity of this issue in practice. The Catholic Christian ideal has to be applied in modern situations when the stresses of modern life, marriage breakdowns, sexual exploitation and medical and economic problems often make it very difficult to implement. A major concern has been widespread poverty and overpopulation in large parts of the world. This has often led to the practice of abortion, which is a moral evil far worse than contraception. Compared with abortion or the breakdown of a marriage, contraception is always the lesser of two evils.

Hence, in practice, the church's pastoral guidance has always to take into account the conscience, the capacities and the social and economic situation of the couple concerned. The following statement from the Second Vatican Council's *The Church in the Modern World* n. 50 sets out the parameters that the Catholic tradition sees as keys to the integrity of sexual activity within marriage:

Married couples should regard it as their proper mission to transmit human life and to educate their children. They should realise that they are thereby co-operating with the love of God the Creator, and are, in a certain way, its interpreters. This involves the fulfilment of their role with a sense of human and Christian responsibility and the formation of correct judgments through docile respect for God and common reflection and effort . . . It also involves a consideration of their own good and the good of their children already born or yet to come, an ability to read the signs of the times and of their own situation on the material and spiritual level, and finally, an estimation of the good of the family, of society and of the Church. *It is the married couples themselves who must in the last analysis arrive at these judgments before God. Married people should realise that in their behaviour they may not simply follow their own fancy, but must be ruled by conscience —* and conscience ought to be conformed to the law of God in the light of the authority of the Church, which is the authentic interpreter of divine law. [Italics added]

The Basic Framework

What we need is a basic framework:
— Which respects the way people feel, think, judge and decide;
— In which all have the task of seeking understanding and deciding;
— Where teachers, directors, facilitators and students all share the task of expressing and supporting their convictions;
— Where the tradition is presented frankly and as clearly as possible;
— Where the faith and convictions of each are acknowledged and respected.

Choosing the framework

There are many different theories of ethics, moral thinking and the valuing process. In this book we have chosen one which has gained wide acceptance. It is based on the work of the philosopher-theologian Bernard Lonergan SJ. We have not tried to apply this theory in a rigid fashion or to follow it point for point, but this is the theory which underlies the process we have developed. From this theory comes the basic four-level approach:

1. Experiencing

I cannot understand until I have some experience to understand. I have to ask: Is it happening? Is it happening to myself, to others? Experience includes people, things I can see, touch, hear around me. It includes behaviour, feelings, emotional responses. This is the raw material of life. Without it we can never reach the level of understanding life. Some experiences are uniquely mine or yours. Some experiences are shared.

2. Understanding

Understanding relates to such questions as: What is really going on? Is it clear? What does it mean? Through understanding we discover what our experience means.

3. Judging

What is really important here? What really matters? What is the truth? Of course, in forming our judgment we have to listen carefully to what others have said about the matter. Unless we listen carefully to others our search for truth would be inadequate. Thus, in this book we have offered some account of what others have said about the most important issues. Judgment often leads to action. This leads to the fourth level — deciding.

4. Deciding

Decisions relate to such questions as: How shall I act? What shall I do? What should I choose? Sometimes a decision is between two contradictory possibilities; sometimes we have to choose from a number of possibilities.

A decision takes what we have experienced, understood and evaluated. It then moves into action. Decisions can be of different kinds:

— Yes or no decision. Do I or don't I?

— Decisions about the best way.

— A decision that I don't yet have enough experience or sufficient understanding to decide. I may have to wait until I have more experience or until I have worked things out more thoroughly. I may have to search out a wider range of opinion.

This book itself is a step in the search for truth. It is part of what has been called 'The never-ending search which every person must undertake for her or himself in order to find out what is worthy and what is not worthy.' This is what we call 'the formation of conscience' (see Chapter 8).

Aims and Prerequisites

In the past the aims of courses in sexuality were often negative. Educators hoped to control sexual expression amongst young people and prevent social problems such as extra-marital pregnancies, sexually transmitted diseases, etc. Often they sought to do this by telling people what is right and what is wrong and how they should behave.

In the previous section we discussed some of the limitations of this indoctrinative method. Our own preference is for an approach which fosters awareness, understanding and a personal search for genuine values. The approach also seeks to respect the values of the tradition to which we are committed. In positive terms, then, our aims can be stated as follows:

* To provide information about sexuality — its social and behavioural aspects as well as biological aspects.
* To assist people to become more aware of their own and other people's attitudes and values concerning sexuality.
* To assist people to be comfortable with their own sexuality, and to be able to talk about sex without guilt and anxiety.
* To help each individual to understand him or herself as a total sexual being and to use that knowledge in a responsible manner.
* To help individuals to examine their attitudes and values in relation to the Church's teaching on sexuality and to arrive at an understanding of the philosophy behind these teachings.
* To foster an awareness of the scriptural foundations of these teachings.

The teacher and the process

The field of sex education is not as straightforward as other areas of education. Teaching about sexuality requires skills other than an ability to impart information. What sorts of skills and qualities are necessary for a good sex educator?

There are a number of issues to consider if you are preparing to undertake sex education courses:

* How aware are you of your own attitudes to sexuality? Think about the ways in which these attitudes may contribute to or interfere with the discussions you will have with young people.
* How comfortable are you with discussion about sexuality? Are you at ease with the use of language about sex?
* We live in a multicultural community in which there is a wide variety of values, attitudes and experiences. How sympathetic are you to variations in values and attitudes? Can you accept differences of opinion? Can you be flexible enough to help people examine values without moralising or condemning? Can you encourage discussion of issues without judgment or criticism of individuals?
* Are you alert to those issues which are potentially sensitive for young people? Can you select approaches to these topics which will support and encourage young people in their understanding and evaluation of issues? This resource

19

book will help you here, but don't underestimate the value of your own ideas.

* Are you familiar with methods and techniques which assist group interaction without forcing involvement or creating a threat?

* Do you have a broad knowledge about sexuality? Are you able to impart information clearly and answer questions adequately? Are you prepared to update your knowledge as new information becomes available?

* Do you have a good knowledge of available resources? Can you use these appropriately to meet your objectives?

These are only a few of the possible issues. What additional issues might you consider? Make your own list of qualities you consider desirable in a good sex educator. Discuss this list with other team members or people working in the field.

Decide what issues you personally will need to work on.

How are you going to go about developing in yourself those skills and qualities you see as desirable?

Remember that the most important qualities you can have are an interest in sex education for young people and a sensitivity to their needs.

Education and training

A variety of courses exist in capital cities and some country centres to assist people to develop their skills in teaching about sex and human relationships. Sources of information in this regard are listed on page 39.

Types of Program

There are a variety of settings in which sex education programs might take place: schools, institutions, church groups, youth groups, training colleges for teachers or nurses and so on. The *type* of program offered will depend very much on the setting. The *content* of the program will be decided according to the needs of participants.

Let us look first at types of programs. In educational institutions there are three main possibilities:

— 'Informal' teaching about various aspects of sexuality and relationships.

— A formal 'short course' in sexuality.

— An 'integrated' approach that educates about sexuality across the curriculum.

In settings other than educational institutions the most likely approach will be the 'short course', but let us look at each possibility in detail.

1. Informal teaching about sexuality

Even in schools where no sex education programs are conducted it is likely that a proportion of class time will be spent examining such issues as:

— family life

— marriage

— relationships

— values.

These issues are all part of education about sexuality. It does not matter whether the learning takes place in English, Social Studies or Religious Education classes. It can still be very worthwhile.

It would be possible to extend the learning possibilities for students by adding to the above list issues such as:

— dating

— communicating with others

— decision-making

— peer group pressure

— male and female sex-roles.

What we are trying to say is that education about sexuality is not just teaching people the facts about genital sex. It is also about exploring relationships and living in the world. So a great deal of appropriate and relevant education can take place informally without calling it 'sex' education or necessitating any formal programming.

In many schools students are receiving education about the biological aspects of sex as part of their courses in science or biology. Again, this informal education about sex can be added to, to explore some issues of greater depth without necessitating a formal 'sex education' program.

2. A formal 'short course' in sexuality

When most people think about sex education they think about

providing a formal course which might cover a number of topics over a limited period of time, say eight or ten sessions.

The temptation here is to limit the material to information about *biological* aspects of sex only, or information about the *Church's teachings* only. Certainly both of these aspects are important for young people, but they are not the only issues. It is preferable for sexuality to be dealt with on a far broader base, taking into account societal pressures, relationships, decision-making and so on. If we isolate sexuality and treat it as a separate dimension, we are making it something unusual or special. Thus we are continuing the myth that sexuality is not something to be accepted and dealt with as part of our ordinary knowledge about human beings, but is somehow 'outside' that knowledge.

A second temptation with the short course approach is to invite outside professionals — medical personnel, trained sex educators — in to conduct the program. Again it is important to consider the effects of this:

— It is likely to identify sexual knowledge as something apart from ordinary knowledge and something which only the medical profession or trained people can handle.

— The guest speakers will not necessarily understand the needs of this particular group of young people. They may well have a prepared course which they conduct irrespective of how relevant it may be.

— The guest speakers will not necessarily have an ongoing relationship with the group. After the course is over participants may have questions, problems or dilemmas which are unresolved. To whom can they take these issues? What is required here is an ongoing relationship between participants and educators so that issues which arise after the course is formally completed can be dealt with easily and comfortably by the same personnel.

What we are saying here is that it is preferable to conduct a sexuality program within an ongoing relationship — e.g. for a class teacher to take the program with his or her own group. This may not be possible in all instances. Some educators are not comfortable with this role. In this case they would be advised to hand over responsibility for the program to someone else.

One should try at all costs to avoid displaying discomfort or embarrassment when discussing sexual topics. Therefore you, the educator, must decide at what level you are comfortable and structure your program around this, inviting other people in to contribute on topics when you consider this necessary.

In many settings it will be possible to operate a team approach, with two or more team members working together on a program, each providing input in his or her own specialist area.

Ideally, team members should include male *and* female educators, working together with the group.

3. An integrated approach that educates across the curriculum

This is the approach we regard as ideal for educational institutions as it enables issues relating to sexuality to be dealt with through different courses, years and levels. For example: in social studies, literature, English, history, science, drama, art, health, etc., issues and topics concerning sexuality can be programmed as part of the course. This approach would require a policy to be formulated for the educational institution and would need ongoing consultation between the teachers involved to ensure that all important issues received attention. Hopefully this approach would be a 'developmental' one, with courses building on the previous year's work and designed to meet the needs of students as they grow in maturity and face different life situations.

Setting up a Program

This book is directed at older adolescents and young adults. There are several ways in which the material could be used:

As a course in sexuality and relationships

The material may be taken as a course handbook and used as the basis for a course in Sexuality and Relationships.

This approach would require approximately 25 to 30 sessions is order to cover the material presented, including activities and discussions. If additional materials are included (such as films, film strips, surveys, other reading matter, etc.) the course would require additional sessions.

As a resource book

The book is structured into 9 work units covering some 24 topics. The material under each topic aims to develop an understanding of that topic through the four-tier approach already referred to:
— Experiencing
— Understanding
— Judging
— Deciding.

Not all the topics will be explicitly broken up in this way. But the four-tier approach remains basic throughout.

The topics are constructed as integrated units in themselves, and may be used independently of each other, or independently of any formal course in sexuality and relationships.

Although some units occasionally cross-reference to others, each unit is in fact independent and can be approached accordingly.

As a reference book or workbook for individuals

The material presented in each unit is very readable in itself and does not necessarily require a group or discussion approach. It can be used as a reference book by individuals. However, there are considerable advantages in a group approach that allows for the sharing of attitudes. Discussion should be encouraged wherever possible.

Providing a program which meets people's needs.

In deciding which approach to use *start with the individual*. Individuals have different needs for information
have different levels of maturity
have different experiences
have different issues they are concerned about.

It is important for facilitators or teachers to be aware of these differences and to build a program of education in sexuality that takes these differences into account.

The contents of this book would best be considered as a resource book for the formation of programs in Sexuality and Relationships. Ideally, programs would use a thematic approach based on participants' expressed needs. There are three levels here:

— Asking participants what they need
— Getting them to tell you what they need
— Providing what they need.

There are issues to be considered at each of these levels.

1. Asking them what they need

There is no point asking people to participate in decision-making unless you are prepared to act on their suggestions.

If you are asking for suggestions about the *content* or *methods* to be used in a program (e.g. which topics they wish to discuss) then you need to make sure that participants are aware of any constraints or external pressures which will limit their choices; for example, the availability of time or resources, the possibility of a veto on parts of the program by some outside authority or the need to obtain parental or institutional approval.

Without this information it is possible that participants will design a program for themselves only to find that what is offered is very different. If this happens they will view the whole exercise as irrelevant, since their expressed needs have been ignored. They may well feel that once again any real discussion of sexual issues is being avoided.

2. Getting people to tell you what they need

Asking people what they need and getting them to tell you are not always the same thing.

Our society has traditionally had strong taboos about sexuality and young people have often learned at a very early age that discussion about sexuality is frowned upon. Many of our educational institutions have reinforced this view by maintaining strict silence on topics related to sexuality. For many

young people sex has been talked about only in contexts which make it appear to be something embarrassing or bad or dirty or funny.

Added to these pressures against open discussion are peer group pressures. If a participant asks for information, perhaps that means he or she 'doesn't know'. Most of us do not like to appear ignorant, particularly in an area as sensitive as sexuality. Therefore, it is common for people to hide the fact that they 'don't know' things they are 'expected' to know by their peers.

For these reasons it is very difficult indeed to encourage people to state what it is they need to know about. And so teachers must be able to:

(a) Create an atmosphere of acceptance of individuals and their contributions.
This will be discussed in detail under 'Group Techniques'.

(b) Create an atmosphere of acceptance of the need for knowledge.
Some techniques which might be useful here are:
— Pointing out that there are several surveys available, the results of which demonstrate the lack of knowledge of most people in the area of sexual information.
— Inviting participants to co-operate in a survey (e.g. questions and answers) to test their knowledge of sexual information. Use the results to point out gaps in knowledge.
— Asking participants to design their own survey on sexual information and sexual attitudes. They could conduct this on their own group or on an outside group of peers.
— Using published information about the *positive* effects of good sex education. Encourage participants to identify areas in which they personally might improve their knowledge or clarify their attitudes. Ask what positive results they might expect for themselves from such things as:
* accurate sexual information
* good decision-making skills
* improved communication skills
* pre-marriage education.
— Using published information about problematic issues such as extramarital pregnancy, marital breakdown, sexually transmitted diseases, etc., to point out the need for information and for good decision-making skills.
Teachers should further be able to:

(c) Conduct the discussion 'one step removed' from the participants.
This allows them to provide input without appearing to talk about themselves. For example:
— Use examples from books or television shows with which they are familiar. Ask questions about the characters: e.g. what sort of relationships are these characters involved in? What pressures are on them? What information would they need to make good decisions for themselves?

— Use examples from participants' past experience: e.g. what sort of information were you given about sex as a child? Who from? What was included or not included? What values were you taught? What negative messages did you get? What positive messages? What things were implied rather than stated directly? What gaps were left for you to fill for yourself later on? What resources were made available to you to fill these gaps in your knowledge? What things are necessary now?
— Talk about the problems of teaching young people about sexuality. Ask them about their perceptions of the role of the family, the school, the Church, in education about sexuality. What difficulties do these groups face in educating young people? Where do these difficulties stem from? What should be done? How? When? What can we do in this context for ourselves and each other?

(d) Encourage work in pairs or small groups

People generally find it far easier to discuss potentially sensitive issues if they are encouraged to do this on a one-to-one or small-group basis. All of the approaches suggested so far could be developed effectively from:
— working in pairs
— then foursomes or small groups
— then the total group.

Individuals find it easier to say: 'In our group we thought . . .' rather than 'I think . . .'

(e) Use written material as a beginning point.

— Use quotes from literature or from the media as a focus for discussion about sexuality and relationships. There are a number of articles in women's magazines and the daily press about sex education, sexual relationships, sexual decision-making and related topics.

The discussion could be directed into questions about *this* group's needs for information.

— Use written material provided by the group members themselves as a basis for discussion, e.g. question box, essays, etc.

— Ask the group to examine a list of topics provided, and rate in order of preference those topics they would like to discuss or have information about.

Some of these methods of information-gathering will do more than just provide information about participants' needs and interests. They will also move participants into beginning to talk about sexuality in a constructive manner. Participants will be feeling more comfortable discussing issues relating to sexuality and using sexual terms. They will have developed a greater degree of interest in the program because of their involvement in planning and thus will have some investment in ensuring the program's success and its relevance to the needs of the group.

3. Providing people with what they need

There are three groups of people you may wish to involve when you are planning your program:
— Parents
— Other staff or team members
— The young people who will be participating.

Parents

If you are working within a tertiary environment or in an independent setting such as a youth group, parent involvement will probably not be a relevant issue. In educational settings such as schools, however, where parental involvement is encouraged, there will already be interaction and discussion between parents and staff on other aspects of the curriculum. It would be a simple matter to extend this discussion to programs concerned with sexuality and human relationships.

In schools where this involvement and interaction does not exist, how best can parents be involved to obtain their support for the program?

Consider first whether you are seeking parental *permission* or parental *support and guidance*. In the school setting sex education, which is the basic right and duty of parents, must always be carried out under their guidance (see *Familiaris Consortio* #37). In all programs openness and collaboration between parents and teachers should be fostered. In some cases it may be sufficient to inform parents of school policy regarding the total curriculum, including courses in sexuality and relationships.

If schools are concerned with the total development of students — psychologically, spiritually, socially, physically and intellectually, then parents may well expect to see human sexuality dealt with as part of the total education process. As it is unwise to separate sexuality education from the total educational program, so it is also unwise to separate it out for parental permission.

This is not to deny the value of seeking parental involvement and support for your program. Nor does it deny a parent's right to withdraw a child of any age from participating in a sex education program. But if you merely ask parents for permission (for example, via a note sent to the home) it is likely that many parents will refuse. Why is this so?

Generally parents have three main anxieties about sex education programs for their children:

* They are worried that their children will have more knowledge about sex than they themselves have.
* They are concerned that the teacher may have different values from themselves.
* They may believe that knowledge about sex will create curiosity about sex — that young people will be likely to experiment with sexual behaviour if they know more about it.

It is possible for the teacher to deal with each of these anxieties in a constructive manner:

— You could provide parents with the same *information* you are planning to give their children. Consider parent education evenings — with films, guest speakers, display of aids, written information and so on. If parents have information about sexuality and are comfortable with language about sex, they may be more prepared to talk about sex with their children themselves. They will certainly be more inclined to support a program about which they have first-hand knowledge.

— Parent education evenings will also provide you with the opportunity to explain the *philosophies and values* underlying your program so that parents are aware of the value base you are working from. You can also encourage parents to share their own values with their children — let them know that they have a right and a responsibility to do this.

— You can inform parents that there is no evidence that sex education programs lead to an increase in sexual experimentation amongst the young. Rather, it appears that young people who are fully aware of the consequences of sexual behaviour are likely to be more responsible in their actions than young people who have little information. It is the latter group who are more likely to experiment out of curiosity.

Once you have reassured parents about the content of your proposed program and the quality of your care and concern for their children, you are in a position to invite more concrete involvement. Let parents know that you welcome their views. You could perhaps call for parental representation on the program planning groups. What about the possibility of community education in sexuality, for home groups or parish groups, etc.?

It is always wise to ensure that you have the full support of your principal and some other staff members. There is always the possibility that some parents will object to your program or to their child's participation in it. This is their right, but it may cause difficulties for you or for the school if you do not have administrative approval and support.

Working with staff or team members
In many instances you will find that other staff members are anxious or unhappy about sexuality education courses for young people. Some of their concerns might be:
— Will I be pressured to be involved?
— Will I be seen as uncooperative if I don't wish to be involved?
— If my views about suitable content or methods for such a program are very different from other people's, will these be heard/accepted/acted upon?
— Will there be negative responses to the program from outside groups such as parents?

If you can be aware of people's concerns in advance you are in a better position to reassure them.

Your main resource in the program will be you, the educator. You need to be seen by staff as someone who is professional in his or her approach. Acceptance of the program will in large part depend on your own credibility. Sometimes it is a good idea for a small group of people to propose a program rather than for one individual to take total responsibility. Working with others in the early stages gives you support and more authority than you might have as an individual.

Consider spending time with people who are experienced in planning and implementing sex education programs. Find out all you can about the resources and the resource people available in your community: approach people for assistance, ask them to act as sounding boards for your ideas. Perhaps invite an outside 'expert' in to work with the staff.

General staff meetings or seminar days may be useful in gaining information about how staff view current needs and problems. These discussions will also provide an opportunity for staff to be reassured about content and methods, and the likely benefits of such a program. Present your material in as positive and non-threatening a way as possible. Report regularly to staff on the progress of the course.

Group techniques: working with young people
Again, your most important resource will be you, the educator. You will need to model positive attitudes about sexuality, and be comfortable talking about issues concerned with sexuality. Your own attitudes and the type of relationship you develop with the group members will be more important than your experience, training or knowledge, although these are very important.

If your goal is to encourage the development of positive attitudes towards others and towards sexuality, you will need to create an atmosphere of acceptance of individuals and their views. Members of the group should feel that their opinion is recognised and their contribution valued. Participants should know that they will not be laughed at, condemned, ignored or punished in any way for expressing their views. Each individual should feel respected as a person.

As a teacher/facilitator you will need to model this respect and acceptance. You may also need to teach group members to provide this acceptance for each other. You can do this by laying down some ground rules for discussion.

It may also be helpful to spend some time with your group practising good discussion technique. Chapter 4 ('Communication') includes some exercises on listening skills which may be helpful here.

Group size will have some bearing on the success of discussion. Where possible, work with small groups rather than large groups or whole classes. Small-group interaction encourages the free exchange of attitudes and ideas. People will generally be more prepared to share their feelings about an issue in a small group.

Groups of five to eight members are an ideal size for discussion. If the group becomes larger than this it is likely that some members will not contribute readily. Sometimes it is useful to work in pairs, before forming into small groups.

All groups require a leader or facilitator who is confident with group discussion techniques, and comfortable with the topic under discussion. If you have more than one group operating, work with other staff or team members, as necessary.

You should not expect group members to always agree, or to come to a consensus on any issue. Nor should they necessarily agree with *you* the educator. The role of the facilitator/leader in a discussion group is not to be an authority on every issue, but to encourage members to participate in the discussion and interact among themselves. If you are expecting group members to agree with your own attitudes and values it is likely that you are moralising or indoctrinating rather than educating. Such an approach will lead to a closing down of discussion and will negate the value of group discussion as a learning experience. The 'values clarification' approach to education about sexuality aims to assist individuals to clarify for themselves what they think. It does not tell them *what* to think.

Obviously, people do not make decisions in a vacuum. They need to have all the relevant factual information. They also need to to know what others think. The 'others' may include peers, parents, teachers, the Church, philosophers, writers, poets, the media, etc. A young person can be encouraged to make decisions on the basis of information available from all of these sources and should have access to all of them.

Again, your own contribution is important here. Always feel free to give your own opinion in any discussion. You too are part of the group and participants will welcome honest contributions from you. If you model openness in that you are prepared to share your opinions and hear and accept other people's opinions, the group participants will be encouraged to behave in the same way.

Being 'open' in a group discussion does not, however, mean sharing intimate details about your personal life or your experiences. Sometimes this sort of sharing can be destructive to your role as a teacher/facilitator. It is also possible that your experiences may be irrelevant to the lives of the young people with whom you are working. Try to achieve a level of openness about your opinions, attitudes, values and feelings which avoids the use of detailed information about yourself and your life. You can also extend this principle to group members, by asking them to discuss 'case histories' or examples from literature or television, rather than their own personal experiences. Unless you are a very experienced group worker you may find it difficult to handle the consequences for individuals if too much personal detail is shared.

Never force people to contribute to the discussion. Where the topic is a potentially sensitive one all participants should feel free to contribute or not, as they wish.

Gender issues

Recent research in education clearly demonstrates the role of the school in transmitting, continuing and reinforcing the dominant values of society, particularly the gender stereotypes and sexual inequalities inherent in our society.

Schools achieve this through the organisation of resources, the construction of curriculum and the covert sexism that occurs almost automatically in mixed-sex groups and which results in the preferential treatment of males.

Although most teachers would strongly argue that they do not discriminate between males and females in classroom behaviour, the evidence exists that discrimination does occur in the interaction that takes place in classrooms and mixed-sex groups. Research shows that girls receive only one-third of the teacher's attention in mixed-sex classrooms, and that males generally control conversations and the topics of discussion (Spender, 1980 and 1982). This has implications for the provision of sex education programs.

It is clear that females will require support in mixed groups if they are to have some control over the content of courses. Females may have different needs for information from males. They may wish to discuss aspects of female sexuality or be particularly interested in communication in relationships. They may have questions about how to get males to take responsibility in relationships. They may wish to develop skills in assertiveness. In mixed-sex groups where males have control of the curriculum these needs are unlikely to be met without intervention from the teacher/facilitator.

Males may view some sex education topics as not relevant to their needs. They will need encouragement to see issues such as conception, birth control, pregnancy and birth, rape and some aspects of relationships as relevant.

Some of these topics could usefully be discussed by single-sex groups prior to, or in addition to, discussion in a mixed group. This would encourage free discussion among young women about topics of concern to them, without fear of embarrassment and without the male domination of discussion which is likely to occur in mixed groups. If handled well, this could also result in young men being challenged to question some of the stereotypes about gender behaviour and may encourage them to take greater responsibility for their own attitudes and behaviour.

Teachers will need to be aware of the changes taking place among some groups in society regarding appropriate gender behaviour. In some social groups within the community female expectations of males and male self-expectations are changing to include an expectation that men and women will share responsibility for communication within the relationship, for initiation of dating and sexual activities, for expression of feelings, for earning income, for child-rearing and housework. In many instances women are seeking satisfaction from a working life outside the home. Some men are becoming more family oriented and more concerned with the nurturing of children and the management of a household.

These changes in gender behaviour have altered our perceptions about what is possible. Many young people are unhappy with the traditional male and female roles. An increasing number of young women are expressing dissatisfaction with the quality of the emotional content of their relationships with men. Men, too, are struggling with new ways of dealing with relationships.

Teachers will want to encourage discussion of these issues.

Resources

In formulating your course you will have become familiar with a wide range of resources available for use in sexuality programs. Choose resources which fit in with the aims and objectives of the course. Before using any audiovisual resource preview the material yourself to ensure that it is appropriate and relevant to your group's needs.

There are a number of films available which can be very valuable as discussion starters. Other films (e.g. human biology films) have a high information content. It is generally preferable to use these films to reiterate information which participants have already learned, rather than as a means of introducing a complex topic.

In addition, encourage group participants to develop their own resource collection. They will have access to libraries, hospitals and community agencies. They can also create their own materials through such methods as imaginative role-plays: writing poems and plays; expression through art-work; undertaking surveys; making strip cartoons; collages, or teaching aids; collecting media articles; making tapes or films.

It is not helpful for young people to see their learning about sexuality and relationships as something separate from the 'real world', so wherever possible resources should link with resources outside the learning environment.

Liaise with other service providers. Arrange visits to community agencies or have speakers on, for example, pre-marriage education programs, marriage, pregnancy, AIDS, sexually transmitted diseases. Utilise community resources which are available to support the program. This will assist in establishing and maintaining consistency between the learning environment and the 'real world' and will provide students with valuable knowledge of community services.

Finally, allow students flexibility to follow up on new issues that emerge from their participation on any topic. Additional learning experiences may need to be provided, such as skills training in communication, assertiveness, or problem-solving, or opportunities for the development of self-esteem.

Evaluation

In all educational programs it is important to build in some method of evaluation. Evaluating the program will help you to see whether you are in fact achieving your aims and objectives.

Your best evaluation will be your own assessment of the interest and involvement of participants. Think about what has happened. Where possible discuss your assessment with other team members. What went well? What went badly? What do you need to change?

Other methods of evaluation include:
— Asking people to write comments on the positive and negative aspects of the program.
— Feedback sessions with participants
— Questionnaires
— Checklist
— Follow-up studies.

The key to positive attitudes about sexuality and relationships is a positive self-concept. We must assist young people to see themselves as worthwhile and valuable human beings, deserving of respect and care, and help them see other people as other 'selves' deserving of the same respect and care. In this way we can promote positive, healthy and responsible attitudes towards sexuality in our society.

Education and Training

You will find it extremely helpful to undertake some formal training program in health education, human relations education or sex education. This will extend your knowledge of resources and your awareness of teaching/learning strategies suited to the diverse needs of young people.

It will also assist you to acknowledge the variety of ways in which different people learn so that you can provide a range of learning opportunities suited to the varying levels of ability or different learning styles of your students.

The course will help you adapt your teaching style to emphasise the active, exploratory and interactive methods most suited to dealing with value clarification and discussion of sensitive topics.

A variety of courses exist in capital cities and some country areas to assist people to develop their skills in teaching about sex and human relationships.

In Australia

The State Education Department — especially the Curriculum Branch.
The Catholic Education Office — especially the Religious Education Branch.
Commonwealth or State Departments of Health — especially the Education Branch.
Tertiary institutions in your area.
The Family Planning Association of Australia.
Local Community Health Centres.

In New Zealand

Christian Family Life Education: 6 Harrow Place, Palmerston North.
National Centre for Religious Studies: 52A Temple St, Meadowbank, Auckland 5.
Diocesan Religious Education Centrēs.
Natural Family Planning Health Care Centres.
Presbyterian Support Services.
Marriage Guidance Council.
Department of Maori and Island Affairs.
Department of Social Welfare.

New Zealand is fortunate to have a network of tutors trained by Christian Family Life Education (CFLE), an institute founded by the New Zealand Catholic Bishops' Conference in 1975–76. Tutors are active in every diocese, and may be located through the National Centre for Religious Studies.

Further reading

1. Strategies for teaching human sexuality courses

BURT, John J. and MEEKS, Linda B. *Education for Sexuality: Concepts and Programs for Teaching*. Holt Rinehart & Winston, New York, 3rd edn, 1985.

CLARITY COLLECTIVE. *Taught Not Caught: Strategies for Sexuality Education*. Spiral, Melbourne, 1983.

CANFIELD, J. and WELLS, H. C. *100 Ways to enhance Self-Concept in the Classroom*. Prentice-Hall, New Jersey, 1976.

FRAENKEL, J. *Helping Students Think and Value*. Prentice-Hall, New Jersey, 1973.

McCARTHY, Wendy. *Teaching About Sex: The Australian Experience*. Allen & Unwin, Sydney, 1983.

STRADLING, R. et al. *Teaching Controversial Issues*. Edward Arnold, London, 1987.

SZIROM, Tricia and DYSON, S. *Greater Expectations: A Source Book for Women's Groups*.

SZIROM, Tricia. *Teaching Gender? Sex Education and Sexual Stereotypes*. Allen & Unwin, Sydney, 1988.

WELLINGS, Kaye. *First Love First Sex: A Practical Guide to Relationships*. Greenhouse Publications, Melbourne, 1986.

WOOD, Jenny. *Health Education Resource Book 3 — Relationships*. Nelson, 1986.

2. Philosophies and values underlying teaching of Christian sexuality

DOMINIAN, Jack. *Proposals for a New Sexual Ethic*. Darton, Longman & Todd, London, 1977.

DOMINIAN, Jack. *Sexual Integrity: The Answer to AIDS*. Collins Dove, Melbourne, 1987.

FOSTER, Richard J. *Money, Sex & Power: The Challenge to the Disciplined Life*. Hodder & Stoughton, London, 1987.

HANNIGAN, James P. *What Are They Saying About Sexual Morality*. Paulist, New York, 1982.

HOGAN, Richard M. and LEVOIR, John M. *Covenant of Love: Pope John Paul II on Sexuality, Marriage, and Family in the Modern World*. Image Book, Doubleday, New York, 1986.

JOHN PAUL II. *Original Unity of Man and Woman: Catechesis on the Book of Genesis*. St. Paul Editions, Boston, 1981.

JOHN PAUL II. *The Family: Domestic Church*. St Paul Publications, 1983.

KEANE, Philip SS. *Sexual Morality: A Catholic Perspective*. Paulist Press, New York, 1977.

KELLY, Kevin T. *Life and Love: Towards a Christian Dialogue on Bioethical Questions*. Collins Flame, London, 1987.

KOSNIK, A. et al. *Human Sexuality: New Directions in Catholic Thought*. Search Press, London, 1977.

LAWLER, Ronald; BOYLE, Joseph; MAY, William E. *Catholic Sexual Ethics: A Summary, Explanation and Defense*. Our Sunday Visitor, Huntington, Indiana, 1985.

LIEBARD, Odile M. (ed.) *Official Catholic Teachings: Love and Sexuality*. Consortium Books, Wilmington, N.C. 1978.

McCARTHY, Donald G. and BAYER, Edward J. *Handbook on Critical Sexual Issues: The Latest Medical-Moral Research on Issues of Human Sexuality and Sexual Issues in Light of the Teaching of the Catholic Church*. Image Book, Doubleday, New York, 1984.

MAY, William. *Sex, Marriage and Chastity: Reflections of a Catholic Layman*. Franciscan Herald Press, Chicago, 1981.

OHANNESON, Joyce. *And They Felt No Shame: Christians Reclaiming Their Sexuality*. Winston Press, Minnesota, 1983.

3. Moral background

GILLIGAN, Carol. *In Another Voice: Psychological Theory and Women's Development*. Harvard University Press, Cambridge, Mass., 1982.

GREEN, Michael et al. *The Church and Homosexuality: A Positive Answer to the Current Debate*. Hodder & Stoughton, London, 1988.

HENNESSY, Thomas C. SJ. *Value/Moral Education: School and Teachers*. Paulist Press, New York, Darton, Longman & Todd, London, 1975.

KIELY, Bartholomew M. SJ. *Psychology and Moral Theology*. Gregorian University Press, Rome, 1980.

KOHLBERG, Lawrence. *Essays on Moral Development, Vol. 1: The Philosophy of Moral Development*. Harper & Row, San Francisco, 1981.

MUNSEY, Brenda (ed.) *Moral Development, Moral Education and Kohlberg*. Religious Education Press, Alabama, 1980.

4. Factual information

BILLINGS, Evelyn and WESTMORE, Ann. *The Billings Method: Controlling Fertility without Drugs or Devices*. Anne O'Donovan, Melbourne, 1982.

BRADFORD, David. *A.I.D.S., Herpes and Everything You Should Know about V.D. in Australia*. Melbourne University Press, Melbourne, 1985.

DIXON, Beverly R. and BOUMA, Gary D. *Personal Development: Health and Human Relations in Australia*. OUP, Melbourne, 1987.

FLYNN, Anna M. and BROOKS, Melissa. *A Manual of Natural Family Planning*. Unwin Hyman, London, 1985.

FOSTER, John L. (ed.) *Unmarried Mothers*. Edward Arnold, London.

FOSTER, John L. (ed.) *You and Your Body*. Edward Arnold, London.

GARDNER-LOULAN, J. et al. *Period*. McPhee Gribble & Penguin, 1984.

HART, John. *Straight Talk About Being Gay*. Penguin, 1986.

KITZINGER, Sheila. *The Experience of Childbirth*. Penguin, 1987.

LANSON, L. *From Woman to Woman* Penguin, 2nd edn, 1983.
LLEWELLYN-JONES, Derek. *A – Z of Women's Health.* OUP, 1983.
LLEWELLYN-JONES, Derek and ABRAHAM, Susan. *Every-girl.* OUP, 1986.
LLEWELLYN-JONES, Derek. *Every Man.* OUP, 1981.
LLEWELLYN-JONES, Derek. *Everywoman.* Penguin, 4th edn, 1986.
LLEWELLYN-JONES, Derek. *Understanding Sexuality.* OUP, 3rd edn, 1988.
MARSHALL, John. *Natural Family Planning.*
McCORMACK, Mary. *The Generation Gap.* Constable, London, 1985.
NILSSON, Lennart. *A Child is Born.* Penguin, 1982.
SHORT, Ray E. *Sex, Dating and Love: 77 Questions Most Often Asked.* Lutheran Publishing House, Adelaide, 1985.
RICHARDSON, Diane. *Women and the AIDS Crisis.* Pandora (Routledge & Kegan Paul), London, 1987.

Resources on AIDS

AIDS Education: Issues and Perspectives for Catholic Schools K–12, Catholic Education Offices of Sydney and Parramatta, 1988. [A comprehensive kit for teachers, parents and students]
'AIDS: A Statement of Pastoral Concern on the AIDS Issue', Advisory Committee on Catholic Social Welfare, Melbourne, 1988.
AIDS: A Time to Care, a Time to Act: Towards a strategy for Australians (A policy discussion paper). Australian Government Publishing Service, Canberra, 1988.
'AIDS: Health Report to the Nation', sponsored by National Advisory Committee on AIDS, Canberra, 1986.
AIDS Virus Infection prepared by Albion Street Centre for the NSW Health Department.
'Care of a Person with AIDS at Home', National Advisory Committee on AIDS, Canberra, 1987.
'Infection Control Guidelines: AIDS and related conditions', AIDS Task Force, Canberra, 1986.
'Facts about AIDS', AIDS Task Force, Canberra, 1986.
HAWKES, Nigel. *AIDS.* Franklin Watts, 1986. [Readable for Years 7–10]
NOURSE, Alan E. *AIDS.* Franklin Watts, 1987. [Teacher and senior secondary reference]
Statement on AIDS by the Australian Catholic Episcopal Conference, 1988.
See also articles in *New Scientist* and *Scientific American.*

5. General texts

BALDWIN, Dorothy. *All About Health: An Introduction to Health Education.* OUP.
GORDON, Sol. *You Would If You Loved Me.* Bantam Books.
GREENWOOD, Judy. *Coping with Sexual Relationships.* Macdonald, Edinburgh, 1984.

HENDIN, Herbert. *The Age of Sensation: A Psychoanalytical Exploration.* W. W. Norton, New York, 1975.

HOLMES, Anna. *Womanhood*, Collins Dove, Melbourne, 1989.

HUNT, Morton M. *The Natural History of Love.* Knopf, New York, 1959.

LEWIS, C. S. *The Four Loves.* Fontana, London, 1969.

MONTGOMERY, Bob and EVANS, Lynette. *Living and Loving Together.* Nelson, Melbourne, 1983.

MUSSEN, KONGER & KAGAN. *Child Development and Personality.* Harper & Row, New York, 6th edn, 1984.

OUTKA, Gene. *Agape: An Ethical Analysis.* Yale University Press, New Haven, 1976.

PIEPER, Joseph. *About Love.* Franciscan Herald Press, Chicago, 1972.

POWELL, John SJ. *Why Am I Afraid to Love?* Fontana, 1975.

POWELL, John SJ. *The Secret of Staying in Love.* Argus, Niles, Illinois, 1976.

POWELL, John SJ. *Through Seasons of the Heart.* Fount, London, 1988.

Audio-visual resources

In Australia

Australian Film Institute (Victoria and NSW)

Catholic Audio-Visual Centre, Homebush, NSW

Family Planning Association of Australia

State Education Department — especially the Curriculum Branch

State Department of Health — especially the Education Branch

State Film Centre — in each State.

In New Zealand

See resource centres listed above under 'Education and Training'.